Awesome Riddles for Kids

Fun Brain Stumpers

For Ages 9 to 12

With
Fun Illustrations

Riddleland

Table of Contents

bonus book

https://pixelfy.me/riddlelandbonus

Thank you for buying this book. As a token of our appreciation, we would like to offer a special bonus - a collection of 50 original jokes, riddles and funny stories.

Introduction

"The more that you read, the more things you will know. The more that you learn, the more places you will go."

~ Dr. Seuss

Thank you for purchasing this book: **Fun Riddles and Trick Questions For Kids – Fun Brain Stumpers for Age 9-12**. During these preteen years, children are transitioning into secondary education and their lives inevitably become busier with homework, clubs, sports, and extra-curricular activities. This is also a time in which children are seeking greater independence. As parents, we devised the book in order to have more enjoyment as a family by asking one another mind-boggling riddles, that are a whole heap of fun. We believe it's really important to set quality time aside to stretch the mind and imagination and build bonds as a family.

As parents, we've found that through fun riddles our children have learned many educational and life-skills without realizing that this crucial learning is taking place. Three of the top skills that we believe riddles promote and encourage are the following:

1. **The Ability to Think Outside the Box:** Riddles help children apply logic and creativity to reach a conclusion. Children can learn literal and non-literal meanings of words. Children can learn to use their imaginations and become more inventive.

2. **Problem Solving:** In order to solve problems, children need to be able to ind solutions, resolve issues, and develop creative options.

3. **Enhancing Vocabulary:** Unfamiliar words present parents with the perfect opportunity to encourage kids to use a dictionary. Parents can then encourage them to use the words in sentences to ensure that they understand their meaning. The riddles will certainly help to place new words in context in a fun way.

The riddles in this book include "Who or what am I?" questions. There are tricky questions that will activate brains. Brief scenarios that are great for problem solving skills ask the question "How did that happen?" The final chapter has clues and anagrams that need unjumbling to give the correct answer; this is great for improving vocabulary and spelling. The book also contains science and nature fun facts. These intriguing facts are often springboards for family discussions.

We hope you and your family have as much fun working through these riddles as our family did. Good Luck!

Chapter 1

Make a Wild Guess

★

"Don't just read the easy stuff.
You may be entertained by it, but you
will never grow from it."

~ Jim Rohn

Chapter 1 - Questions

Take your time going through each question. If you feel that you are unable to solve a question, then move on to the next. One of the best ways to answer riddles is by making as many guesses as possible. It does not matter if you are making the wrong guess. What matters is that you are slowly removing the wrong answers one by one until you arrive at the correct answer.

1. Sometimes, I am able to dig tiny caves. When I do, I store silver and gold in them. I can also use silver to build bridges and gold to make special crowns. However, the bridges and crowns are truly small! Many people come to me with their troubles.

Who am I?

2. I am made of fire, so you can't touch me. I give off heat, but you can't see me in the dark.

What am I?

3. I can fly, but I do not have wings. I can carry, but what I carry are not objects. I am a leader, but I am not a king. I navigate, but I am not a sailor.

Who am I?

Chapter 1 - Questions

4. I am white, but I am not snow. I can grind and cut, but I am not a knife. The lion has me, but the turtle does not. You have me, but the parrot does not.

What am I?

5. When I expand, I take in something. When I contract, I remove something. I am found within your body and I am important for your life.

What am I?

6. You can hold me in your other hand, but you cannot hold me in the same hand. I always appear at a bend and I help a part fold.

What am I?

7. I am created inside you and there are many of me. I carry an important fluid all around your body.

What am I?

8. I am someone who grows old. There is no one else like me. I can sing, walk, dance, and think. I can build things and I can dream big. I am capable of achieving so many wonderful things.

Who am I?

Chapter 1 - Questions

9. I am able to show how hot it can be, but I can also be something that floats and that you can't see.

What am I?

10. I am four feet tall, but do not mistake me for a human being! I can stand in water, but I prefer it to be shallow. I am quite pink, and I have wings.

What am I?

11. I am always finding new things and proving theories. When I am not looking at tiny objects, I am looking at gigantic ones.

Who am I?

FUN FACT

Did you know that the largest living organism is a fungus named Armillaria ostoyae? If you can't pronounce that word, then perhaps you can use its other name Humongous Fungus!

Chapter 1 - Questions

12. Sometimes I carry secrets, and at other times I carry objects. People even use me to send messages. I don't go anywhere randomly. I usually have a destination to reach.

Who am I?

13. I am quite light, and I can fill up a balloon. I am the second one in my group.

What am I?

14. I am not a king. I am not an actor, and I am not a tailor. Yet, I hold many clothes.

What am I?

15. Am I not curious? Well, I am. I am capable of raising doubts. I am also capable of making sure that something is right. I am important if you want to ask someone whether they are right or wrong. I am also important during an exam.

What am I?

16. I am able to grow even though I am not alive. I need air even though I do not have a mouth. I disappear if you add water to me.

What am I?

17. The mind is a mysterious place, and I like to understand it. But I understand the mind because I want to understand people.

Who am I?

Chapter 1 - Questions

18. People eat one but throw away two. I am found in the sea, but not on land.

What am I?

19. I can be quite dangerous, but I am not bacteria. In fact, I am nearly 100 times smaller than bacteria.

What am I?

20. You can play me. You can tell me. You can make me. You can crack me.

What am I?

21. Animals are great, so I study them. I like to classify and understand their behavior.

Who am I?

22. I can sometimes laugh, and I can sometimes cry. I have so many different expressions. I can turn into a vegetable, or I can even turn into an animal. I am all inside your smartphone.

What am I?

FUN FACT

Did you know that a crocodile
cannot stick its tongue out?

23. I am usually dressed in white, but I don't wear a suit. Some people offer me a carrot, but I don't eat it. Some people even offer me pieces of wood, but I don't burn them. If it's hot, you won't find me. If it is cold, you may make me.

Who am I?

24. I can soar into the sky. I can fight dragons. I can become anyone you want me to be. Yet, I am always within you.

What am I?

25. I can be many colors, but I am not a leaf. I am able to imitate others, but I am not a monkey.

What am I?

Chapter 1 - Questions

26. I have many hands, but I cannot move them. I have a large crown, but it is not made of metal. I even have many legs, but they are underground.

What am I?

27. I study how organisms are related to the environment. I am closely related to the word biology.

Who am I?

28. I look like water, and I simmer like heat. I can lie on the sand, and I can lie on concrete. When I appear, people follow me everywhere. When they don't reach their destination, all they can do is stare.

What am I?

Chapter 1 - Questions

29. I float in the sky, but I am not a plane. I am white, but I am not snow.

What am I?

30. If you do not measure me, then you won't be able to know I am there. Yet when I fly by, you miss me.

What am I?

31. You can touch me, but you cannot see me. You can put me down, but you can't throw me away.

What am I?

FUN FACT

A lightning bolt can be five times
hotter than the surface of the sun!

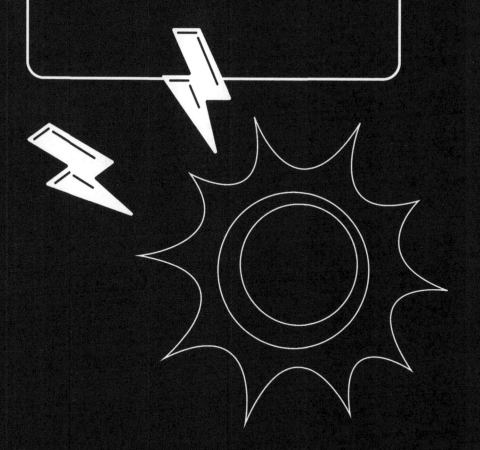

32. I run into a city. I run out of the city. I do this all the time even when you are not looking at me.

What am I?

33. I may have a tiny eye and a slender body, but you will never see me cry.

What am I?

34. I have six letters. But, if you were to remove one, then I become 12.

What am I?

35. No one has seen me, but I always happen. I am never in the past, and I am always present in the future.

What am I?

36. You may see me all around a farm, but you will never see me move.

What am I?

37. I may have no wings, no hands, and no feet, but I can still reach the sky.

What am I?

38. The more of me you take, the more of me is present behind you.

What am I?

39. I can be flat, or I can be wavy. I can be shallow, or I can be deep. I can carry many objects while other objects can flow through me.

What am I?

Chapter 1 - Questions

40. Do you love rocks? Well, I do. I study them. More importantly, I study the matter that makes up the earth.

Who am I?

41. I have nine bodies within me, but none of them are living. They do move around, but they do not have any legs. They float, but they are not fish. Recently, someone told me that I actually have eight!

What am I?

42. I am found outside your mind but under your face. I may cover your thoughts, but your appearance covers me.

What am I?

43. I grant you access to treasures. I let you enter homes. With just a twist, I can remove strong binds.

What am I?

44. I meow like a cat. I even look like a cat. Yet, I am not a cat.

What am I?

FUN FACT

Did you know that snails can sleep for as long as 3 years?

Chapter 1 - Questions

45. To open me, you need a key. The key is one that is not made using a locksmith's hand, but it is one only I am able to understand.

What am I?

46. I am three, but I am all the same. You can call me, but you need to use different names. I can play and I can walk. I can sing and I can talk.

What am I?

47. If you guide me, I scrape. If you don't, I lie still. The more of me you use, the less of me you will have.

What am I?

48. If you want me, then you usually have to give me. The old need me, and certain people demand me.

What am I?

49. I am usually red, yellow, and brown. I come in different shapes depending on what type I come from. I am found on the ground after falling and I'm great fun to kick up.

What am I?

50. I have a thin body and many feathers. I can fly, yet I am not alive. My head is sharp.

What am I?

51. Twelve of me make a whole. You can count me, but you cannot hold me.

What am I?

52. You can let me fall from the tallest of buildings, and I will still survive. Yet if you place me on water, I slowly begin to disappear.

What am I?

Chapter 1 - Questions

53. I am right, but I am never wrong.

What am I?

54. When you pronounce me, I don't sound like a word at all.

What am I?

55. I am a bag, but you put me in boiling water. The longer I am in the water, the more you are able to taste.

What am I?

56. I am unique at first, but then I become the same. I am a key, but I don't open physical locks.

What am I?

57. If you rearrange the letters OWONDER, then I become one word.

What am I?

FUN FACT

Did you know that dogs have two air passages? They use one air passage for breathing and the other for smelling. This means that they can smell even when they are exhaling!

58. I have four siblings, and I am the shortest. Yet, among all the siblings, I am the strongest. I can be "OK." Or, I can be "Not OK."

What am I?

59. You can find me on someone's face. You may find me in someone's speech. I can spread love, or I can spread sadness. I can be angry, or I can be funny.

What am I?

60. I sit in parliament, but I am not an important person. I work during the night, and I rest during the day.

What am I?

61. I am always passing in front of the sun, yet I never create a single shadow.

What am I?

62. I am always in place, but I am never in everywhere. I am always the first in my group. You can find me in cars, but not in buses.

What am I?

63. I have two eyes and one nose. I have 10 fingers and 10 toes. I am beside you, but not always physically. I help you sometimes emotionally.

What am I?

64. I have a small house, but there are no doors or windows. If I want to get out, I might have to break the walls.

What am I?

65. You may not be able to see me, but guess what? I can see through you!

What am I?

66. Sometimes, I am easy to find, but sometimes I am not. I have so much information to tell you. I can speak about the universe, and I can speak about animals. In fact, I can speak about almost anything you are curious about.

What am I?

FUN FACT

Did you know that there is an animal called beefalo? It is half cow and half bison.

67. I take away the bad, and I take away the old. I am a filter and cannot fold. I am shaped like a bean, but you cannot eat me.

What am I?

68. I hold a thousand wheels, but I don't move at all. There may be plenty of me, or there may be little. I may be a building, or I may be on the road.

What am I?

69. I make sounds and I create waves. I can make you jump, and I can make you sleep. You can create me on your own, or you can create me in a group.

What am I?

70. You have me, but animals don't. Famous people have me, but some of them don't. You can find me in Bill Gates, but you cannot find me in Beyonce.

What am I?

71. If you do not know what I am, then I can be quite puzzling. But when you know what I am, then I am reduced to nothing.

What am I?

72. I am two in a person and five in an individual. I am two in a human but three in an animal.

What am I?

73. I roam in the sky like a cloud. I am fast, but I am not loud.

What am I?

74. I have just one head and one foot, but as long as you want me, I never get tired of dancing.

What am I?

75. I can be quite thin when I am empty. But when I am full, I am as big as what is inside me.

What am I?

76. I can be inside, and I can also be outside. I can hold kings and queens, and I sometimes have a screen. People can walk on me, or people can talk on me.

What am I?

77. Everyone has me even though they deny I exist. You can create me, but you cannot hold me for long.

What am I?

78. I am not flora; I am fauna. I am not a tree, but I am foliage. I am not grass.

What am I?

79. I have a red coat and I also have a stone in my throat.

What am I?

FUN FACT

It takes an entire month for
a sloth to move one mile.

80. I am happening to everyone at the same time. No matter what you do, I always happen.

What am I?

81. There are billions and billions of me spread out in a really large space. In each one of me, you find billions and billions of moving objects. If you need to see me, then you might need a special object.

What am I?

82. I have red. I even have blue and green. Oh, look! I do have orange as well. Yet, I do not have gold.

What am I?

83. I do not have legs or eyes. But, I am so strong that I can move earth.

What am I?

84. I may be red, but I can be green as well. Sometimes, I can be yellow. You can definitely eat me.

What am I?

85. I have 16 that go front and back. I am there to protect the King from an attack.

What am I?

86. I contain a whole village or city. When you use me, you have control over the weather.

What am I?

87. You give me to other people, but you still have to keep me.

What am I?

88. I do not have arms or legs. I do have a long body and teeth.

What am I?

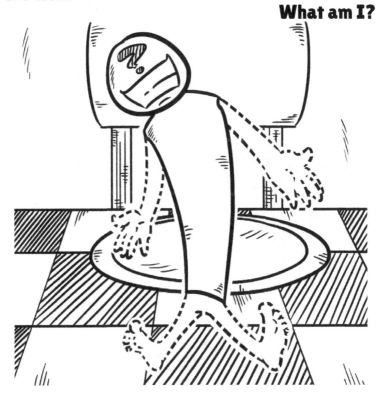

89. Many nights I go over the hills and fly over the willows. I have a strong bite, but I never swallow.

What am I?

90. I can go from one house to the other. I am sometimes wide, and sometimes I am narrow. Whether it rains or snows heavily, I am always found outside.

What am I?

FUN FACT

There is a hurricane on Jupiter that has been going on for 300 years!

Chapter 1 - Questions

91. I may be negative, but I am not an emotion. I may be negative, but I am not a number. I may be negative, but I am not the temperature. I may be negative, but you cannot see me.

What am I?

92. I am the yesterday of tomorrow and the tomorrow of yesterday.

What am I?

93. I may go up and I may go down, yet I do not take a single step at all. People need me to reach something and people need me to get down.

What am I?

94. I can show you sweetness. I can show you bitterness. I can show you sourness. But, guess what. I am not your emotions.

What am I?

95. I am a house that has two occupants. Sometimes, there is just one, but rarely do you find three. You actually break my borders and eat the occupants inside!

What am I?

96. I am always around, but you can never reach me. At one point, you used to live within me.

What am I?

97. I end the night and begin the day. If you don't have me, then you are going to pay. I am yours to keep, and sometimes, you may find me while counting sheep. I can come quickly, or I can come slowly.

What am I?

98. Sometimes I cry and sometimes I laugh. I can be a superhero and I can also be a supervillain. I can even be the President! But who I am is left to the imagination.

Who am I?

Chapter 1 - Questions

99. I create sounds, but only when you allow me to. I am used to form words and I am used for blowing air. I am always with you.

What am I?

100. I cut hair and I shave several times every day. Yet, I still end up growing hair by the end of the day.

Who am I?

101. I am something that the rich need and the poor have. I am bigger than infinity and I am present in atoms. Space has me and I am also there if you don't do anything.

What am I?

FUN FACT

The opposite sides of a dice always add up to the number 7.

Chapter 1 - Questions

102. I may be called a building block, but I am not something you can hold in your hands. I am something present INSIDE your hands and in many places inside your body. Who you are is because of what I tell you to be.

What am I?

103. I am a word that has five letters. I start a sequence, and I let everyone know that they should act. Sometimes, people announce me with a gong. I don't end with an out; I and with an in.

What am I?

104. Some people like to think of me as a source of fuel, but I don't power vehicles. People usually have me when they wake up. Many people have me numerous times during the day.

What am I?

105. Some people love me, especially those who are young. Other people dislike me, especially those who are old. I may be hard to forget, but I am sometimes hard to remember. If you do remember me, then you bring many people together to get to know me. But, whether you remember me or not, I am always present year after year.

What am I?

Chapter 1 - Questions

106. I can shine and twinkle, but I am not a star. You can hold me in your hand, but you cannot break me easily. I am possibly the strongest object you know.

What am I?

107. Alone, I can create something strong. Together with two more particles, I am something you breathe out. I am quite important for living things.

What am I?

108. I make a loud roar, but I am not an animal. I start from the top and end up at the bottom. Where I fall is a large pool of water.

What am I?

Chapter 1 - Questions

109. They say that I am unique and one of a kind. There are many like me, but they don't look exactly like me. I am found when the weather gets chilly. I don't go up, but I do fall down.

What am I?

---

110. I am really useful to you if you want to get to the result. You need me to look for things and you need me to measure things as well. If you take away the last two letters in my word, then I become a piece of wood.

What am I?

---

111. I am capable of burning the eyes. I am capable of stinging the mouth. You will find me out at sea. I may have many particles, but I can become part of something else.

What am I?

---

112. I am a number. But even if you spell me, I remain the same.

What number am I?

---

113. On this planet, there is plenty of me. But outside this planet, there is little of me. You need me to move and you can feel it when I touch your face.

What am I?

FUN FACT

There are more sheep in
New Zealand than there
are people.

114. I have two faces, but I have only one head. I may not have any legs, but I can travel quickly. I am real, but I can also be virtual. **What am I?**

115. I have many twists and turns. But, I have no curves. If you twist me the right way, then you can fix me. But if you turn me the wrong way, then you can ruin me.

What am I?

116. I like to rotate my body, but I only do it if it means I am going into something or getting out of something. Though my body twists, my head is always held up high.

What am I?

FUN FACT

Some queen bees can actually
make quacking noises!

Chapter 1 - Questions

117. I grow up and I make people taller. I help some people grow up more than others, while there are other people who don't grow up as much.

What am I?

---

118. I appear when you go from here to there, but I disappear when you go from there to here.

What am I?

Chapter 1 - Answers

1. A Dentist
2. The Sun
3. A Pilot
4. A Tooth
5. Lungs
6. Elbows
7. Red Blood Cells
8. You

9. Mercury
10. A Flamingo
11. A Scientist
12. A Mailman
13. Helium
14. A Clothesline
15. A Question
16. Fire

17. A Psychologist
18. An Oyster
19. A Virus
20. A Joke
21. A Zoologist
22. An Emoji
23. A Snowman
24. Imagination

---

25. A Parrot
26. A Tree
27. A Biologist
28. Effects of a mirage
29. A Cloud
30. Time
31. I am your back.
32. A Road

33. A Needle
34. The word "dozens"
35. Tomorrow
36. Fence or fences
37. Smoke
38. Steps

39. Water. Acceptable answers: ocean, sea, lake, or pond
40. A Geologist
41. The Solar System
42. A Skull
43. A Key
44. A Kitten

---

45. A secret code
46. People who are triplets
47. Chalk
48. Respect, or the ability to give respect
49. Leaves on the ground. Acceptable answer: leaves during autumn.

50. An Arrow
51. A year
52. Paper
53. A right angle
54. An entire sentence
55. Tea bag
56. A Password
57. If you rearrange the letters, then you can form "One word."

58. A Thumb
59. Human emotions
60. An Owl. A group of owls is called a parliament
61. Wind
62. The letter "a"
63. I am your friend.
64. Chicken. Acceptable answers: chick or chicken/ chick in an egg

Chapter 1 - Answers

65. An X-Ray

66. Knowledge

67. A Kidney

68. A Parking Lot

69. Music

70. A last name

71. A Riddle

72. Syllables that make up a word

73. A swarm of birds

74. A spinning top

75. A Bag

76. A stage where you hold plays

77. The feeling of fear

78. A Bush

79. A Cherry

80. Growing older

81. Galaxy

82. A Rainbow

83. A Worm

84. An Apple

85. A game of chess

86. A Snow globe

87. Your word

88. A Fork

89. Frost

90. A Path

91. An Electron

92. Today

93. Stairs

94. Taste buds. Acceptable answer: tongue

95. A Peanut

96. Yesterday

97. Sleep

98. An actor or actress

99. A Mouth

100. A Barber

101. Nothing

102. DNA

103. The word "begin"

104. Coffee

105. A Birthday

106. A Diamond

107. Carbon

108. A Waterfall

109. A Snowflake

110. Logic

111. Salt

112. The number four

113. Air

114. Money

115. A Rubik's cube

116. A Screw

117. Height

118. The letter "T"

Chapter 2

Be Careful!
I am Tricky!

★ ★

"Nothing is particularly hard if you break it down into small jobs."

~ Henry Ford

Chapter 2 - Questions

All the questions under "Tricky Questions" require your imagination. You don't have to pick up a pen and paper in order to write down something; although, you can if you think it might help you reach the answer more quickly. All you need to do is read the questions carefully and use your imagination! After all, the answer might just be staring you in the face.

1. You have a pocket. It has nothing in it, yet it still has something. How is that possible?

2. Harry had stepped out into the rain. He did not have an umbrella with him. He wasn't wearing a hat or a raincoat. But, not a single hair on his head was wet. Why?

3. These letters are found in every day of the week. What letters are they?

4. There are two sons and two fathers in a car. But, there are only three people in total. How is that possible?

5. Draw a line. Without touching this line, how can you make it longer?

6. There is something that you can break even if you don't touch it or pick it up. What is it?

7. Sarah threw a ball as hard as she could. Yet, after travelling a certain distance, it returned to her. How did that happen?

8. How is it possible for you to add two to eleven and still get 1 for the answer?

Chapter 2 - Questions

9. What word in the English language contains two C's, two S's, and two L's?

10. A boy was given a question that he could not answer "yes" to. What question is that?

11. No matter who you are, you will have to take off your hat for one person. Who is that person?

12. There is a nine-letter word that remains a word each time you take away a letter. What word is that?

13. In the land of yellow glass doors, you can find books, but you cannot find televisions. You can find streets, but you cannot find buildings. What is it that you can find in the land of yellow glass doors?

14. There is something that is used by other people very much, but it only belongs to you. What do you think that is?

15. Which of the following birds do not fit in the group? Gull, Finch, Ostrich, Eagle, and Sparrow

FUN FACT

If you are an astronaut and you are in your space station, you will be able to see nearly 16 sunrises and 16 sunsets every day!

Chapter 2 - Questions

16. If the day before yesterday was the 22nd, then what is the day after tomorrow?

17. There is a word that begins with the letter "I." You can add one letter to it, and you still pronounce it the same way. However, the meaning of the word changes. Do you know this word?

18. This word has six letters. However, the 2nd, 4th, and 6th letters are the same. The first letter is the fourth in the series. The third letter is the first one in the word that means the opposite of winning. The fifth letter is something that you can drink as well. What is the word?

19. If you take a hydrogen atom and then fuse it with a helium atom, what are the chances of the neutron having a positive charge?

20. Imagine that you are in the middle of an ocean. There is no land nearby and your boat has a hole. Water is quickly entering the boat and sharks are all around you. What do you do?

21. This is a six-letter word. The first three letters spell out a type of vehicle. The last three letters spell out a creature that you can keep at home. Yes, that creature is friendly. What is the word?

Chapter 2 - Questions

22. You have three oranges in a bowl. You take away two. How many do you have now?

23. A girl first turned right. Then she turned left. She then performed a backflip and turned around. After that, she performed a spin and turned right twice before 1taking a picture of the sunset. What direction was she facing?

24. How many bricks do you think is needed to complete a building that is made entirely of bricks?

Chapter 2 - Questions

25. I am a person, but I am also a fruit and a bird. How can that be?

26. Take a look at these letters. They do not refer to just one word, but an entire phrase. What do you think the phrase is? PAWALKRK

27. A man walked into a police station. Without informing anyone, he walked straight to the elevators and all the way to the third floor. How is that possible?

28. Jennifer, Elizabeth, and Peter are drinking tea. Dave, Amber, and Fred are drinking coffee. What is Louie drinking?

FUN FACT

About 55 million years ago, palm trees used to grow at the North Pole.

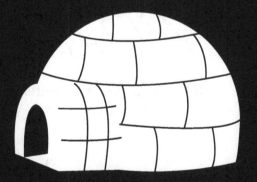

Chapter 2 - Questions

29. What is the missing letter in this sequence of letters? MTWT_SS.

30. What month in the year has 28 days?

31. If you add two letters to a particular five-letter word, it becomes shorter. What word is that?

32. Can you list three days that appear one after the other? You cannot use any of the days in the week.

Chapter 2 - Questions

33. A man was lost at sea. He looked up at the sky and immediately knew which direction he should head toward. How is that possible?

34. What do you think is at the end of a rainbow?

35. There was a plumber, a carpenter, and a teacher walking down the road. Who among them had the biggest hat?

36. Horses have something that no other animal has. What is it?

Chapter 2 - Questions

37. What is the next letter in this sequence?
JFMAMJJASON

38. Mt. Everest is the highest mountain in the world. Before it was discovered, which was the highest mountain in the world?

39. Wednesday, Adam, and Jack went to a restaurant and enjoyed a nice dinner. When the bill arrived, it was paid. However, neither Adam nor Jack paid the bill. Who did?

40. All the members of the Smith family were not able to stand underneath the umbrella. Yet, none of them got wet. How is that possible?

FUN FACT

If you were given the power to continuously ride your bicycle to the moon, it would take you three years to reach it!

3 years

Chapter 2 - Questions

41. There is a word in the English language that follows the rules below. :

    a. The first two letters indicate a man.

    b. The first three letters indicate a woman.

    c. The first four letters refer to a brave man.

    d. The entire word refers to a brave woman.

42. There is a four-letter word that has only two letters. If you read it backward, it reads the same. But, here is the best part; if you flip it over, it still reads the same. What is the four-letter word?

43. A man is trapped inside a room that has only two exits. Behind one door is a giant magnifying glass that is magnifying the hot rays of the sun. If the man opens the door, then he will surely burn. Behind the second door is a fire-breathing dragon. How does the man escape the room?

44. There is a vehicle that is spelled the same backward as it is spelled forward. What vehicle is that?

45. There is a word that begins with the letter "E." However, it can have only one letter in it. How is that possible?

Chapter 2 - Questions

46. How many times can you subtract the number 5 from 100?

47. Tim watched as a tsunami came closer and closer to him. But, nothing happened to his home or the nearby area. How is that possible?

48. This is a fairly odd paragraph. You might look at it and not know why it is odd. But, you have to know that it is odd. It looks so plain. What is so odd about it? You think and think and still do not know why. But, I am still asking you. Why is it odd?

Chapter 2 - Questions

49. A ship was in the middle of the ocean. There seemed to be nothing but water all around the boat. There were two people who were standing on opposite sides of the boat. Surprisingly, the two people could still see each other. How is that possible?

50. I am a word. The first three letters refer to an object that can easily open locks. The last five letters refer to a flat surface. If you combine me, then I refer to something that has many letters and symbols. What word is referred to in this question?

51. What is 1/4 Leek, 2/5 onion, 1/9 drumstick, and 2/5 onion?

52. I am a word. The first four letters refer to something that is white and soft. The last four letters refer to something that is round and can roll on the ground. Together, I become something that people love to play with. What word is referred to in this question?

53. Take a look at the following words and try to see what they might be saying. MCE MCE MCE

54. It takes 10 cats 10 minutes to catch 10 mice. Based on that logic, how long will it take 1 cat to catch just 1 mouse?

Chapter 2 - Questions

55. You have an empty box with you and 20 apples. How many apples can you fit into the empty box?

56. A man named Albert has four sons. Each of those sons has one sister. How many children does Albert have?

57. There is one word that is spelled wrong in each and every dictionary out there. What word is that?

58. Jen added something to her wooden box to make it lighter. What did she add?

59. There is a word in the English language from which you can remove four of its five letters and still pronounce the word in the same way. What is this word?

60. There is a seven-letter word that is pretty heavy. If you remove two letters, it becomes eight. What word am I talking about?

61. A boy has no special powers, but he can predict the score of any football game even one day in advance! How is that possible?

62. A young girl took something, removed the outside, and then cooked the inside. After that, she ate the outside and then threw away the inside. What is the something that the girl took?

63. Look at the arrangement of letters below. They mean something. What are they trying to tell you?

    a. Y   **b.** R   **c.** R   **d.** U   **e.** H

64. The letters below may be rearranged, but they all mean the same thing. Can you figure out the phrase?

    a. e s g g   **b.** g g s e

    c. g s g e   **d.** e g s g

FUN FACT

There is a coral reef shaped like
a heart in Australia.

Chapter 2 - Questions

65. An apple is 5 dollars, a strawberry is 10 dollars, and an orange is 6 dollars. How much is a banana?

66. A boy was about to create words on a page without using pen, ink, or even a computer. How was he able to do that?

67. Scientists have shown that one side of the cat has more hair than the other. Which side is that?

68. I had taken part in a bicycle race. Just before the finish line, I had passed the cyclist in second place. In what place did I finish the race?

Chapter 2 - Questions

69. A boy was able to read with his eyes closed. How is that possible?

70. There are two horses in front of two horses. Then there are two horses behind two horses. You can also find two horses beside each other. How many horses are there in total?

71. A man walked all day but only moved 2 feet. How is that possible?

72. What does this sequence of letters say? KOOL

73. A young man went to the king to ask for his help. The king said that he will help the young man, but only under one condition. Two pieces of paper were shown to the man. Under one was the word "YES" and under the other was the word "NO." In front of a large crowd, the young man needed to pick the "YES" paper. The young man knew that the king was sly and that both papers contained the word "NO." But, the young man still got the king's help. How was he able to do that?

74. How can you change the word DINER into MENUS by only changing one letter at a time? Bear in mind that each time you change a letter, it should change into another English word.

75. A small ball rolled into a hole. This particular hole is quite deep. You cannot put your hands into it and then reach for the ball. There is also a bend in the middle, which means you cannot use a stick or other tools to dig the ball out. The hole itself is made of concrete, so you cannot dig into it. How do you get the ball out?

76. You find yourself locked in a bathroom. The tap is running, and water is quickly filling up the bathtub. Eventually, water will fill the room. You find that the handles to the tap have come off. The doors and windows are locked. Yet the water never rises. How is that possible?

FUN FACT

The reason we have so many seasons is that the Earth is tilted. If the Earth wasn't tilted, then we wouldn't have summer, winter, spring, and autumn.

77. A rooster climbs on top of a roof and lays an egg. Which direction does the egg roll?

78. Which of the following plural forms of animals is incorrect? Tigers, lions, cats, deers, giraffes, monkeys, and cheetahs.

79. Jimmy was holding water in his hands, yet none of the water fell to the ground. How is that possible?

Chapter 2 - Questions

80. A father wanted to reward one of his three children with lots of gold! So, he gave them a test. He gave them a small amount of money and told them to buy something that could fill up an entire room. Susan, the eldest, bought lots of straw, but it wasn't enough to fill up the room. John, the middle child, bought water, but he was still not able to fill the room. Peter, the youngest, bought two items and he successfully filled the entire room with something. The father gave him the gold. What two things did Peter buy?

81. You can fly from Earth to Pluto in just four hours. How is that possible?

Chapter 2 - Questions

82. Without using the internet or a calculator, can you guess how many seconds there are in a year?

83. You have nine toothpicks with you. How can you use them to make ten without breaking any of the toothpicks?

84. What does this sequence of words say? GIVE, GIVE, GIVE, GIVE

85. Ella dropped a ring into some coffee. Surprisingly, the ring did not get wet. How is that possible?

86. You have entered a town where there are only two barbers. They are on opposite sides of the street. The barber on the right has a bald patch on his head. The barber on the left has shiny and well-done hair without a single bald patch. Which barber do you choose?

87. Tom added salt, sugar, and oil to water, but he was not able to mix them all well. Why is that?

FUN FACT

Guess how many seconds
there are in a year?
There are

31,556,926
seconds

Chapter 2 - Questions

88. There was a man who was driving a car. His lights were turned off and the moon was not out yet. A turtle was on the road in front of him and he was able to see it. How is that possible?

89. There were two cars driving on the same road. Both started at the same time - 2:00. One car was heading north while the other car was heading south. Each car was moving in the direction toward the other car. Yet, they did not crash into each other. How is that possible?

90. What are the two things that you can never have for breakfast?

91. A young girl is walking home with a doctor. The girl is the doctor's daughter, but the doctor is not her mother. Who is the doctor?

92. There was a man who ran through a stop sign. Two police officers were nearby, but they did not chase the man. Why is that?

93. Amber loves to eat peas, but she doesn't like potatoes. She enjoys squash, but she hates strawberries. Based on the information that you have, do you think Amber likes apples or pumpkins?

Chapter 2 - Questions

94. When the pig looked up at the sky, it began to count stars. However, that is not possible. Why?

95. Which of the following creatures do not fit in the group? Crocodiles, Turtles, Salamanders, Snakes

96. Mark said to his friend Adam, "I want to listen to dolphins sing." Adam replied, "That is not possible." Why did Adam say that?

97. How can you take something that slips between your fingers to make something that is transparent?

Chapter 2 - Questions

98. One astronaut said to another, "If we start drifting apart, then just shout for me." However, that is not possible. Why is that?

99. John was holding something in his hands. It had little life left in it. But within just a few minutes, it received life. Within a couple of hours, it had come back to life completely. It seemed like a miracle. What power does John have?

100. A young girl was browsing books in a library. After a while, she walked up to the counter. The person behind the counter said, "That will be 8 dollars please." The girl paid the money and walked out of the library without the book. The person behind the counter did not say anything to stop her. Why is that?

FUN FACT

In just the past 5 minutes alone,
Earth has travelled nearly
8,000 kilometers through space!

Chapter 2 - Questions

101. A professor said that all she needed were the three primary colors of red, yellow, and green to make many other colors. She was wrong. Why is that?

102. There is a family of five who lives on the 10th floor of a building. Every day, when the youngest son has to go to school, he uses the elevator to get to the ground floor. But when he returns from school, he uses the elevator to only get to the 5th floor. He then takes the stairs to climb the remaining floors. Why is that?

103. John let the cat out of the bag, yet there was no paper or plastic bag, and nothing furry making a "meow" noice. What did he do?

Chapter 2 - Questions

104. A man was walking home from work. He looked up in the sky to see a beautiful full moon. He turned his head and looked down. Lo and behold! He saw the moon there as well! How is that even possible?

105. Adam jumped off a cliff. He was getting closer and closer toward the ground, but just before he could reach it, he was suddenly pulled back because of a strange force. He fell toward the ground again, but once again, he was pulled back. Eventually, he returned back to the cliff. What did Adam do or what force helped him return safely back to the cliff?

106. There were two people who were born at the same moment. However, they do not share the same birthday. How is that possible?

Chapter 2 - Questions

107. There was an immortal man who was born in 1995. In 1996, he officially celebrated his 3,991 birthday! How is that even possible?

108. A woman decided to describe her daughters. She says that all of her daughters are brunette except one. All of her daughters are blonde except one. All of her daughters are redheads except one. How many daughters does the woman have?

109. There is a house that has four walls. All the walls are facing south. A bear is slowly walking toward it. What color is the bear?

Chapter 2 - Questions

110. If you write every number from 400 to 500, how many times will you have written the number 4?

111. Jim and his friend Benny were rolling dice. Suddenly, Jim said, "I want die." The two friends continued to play and nothing happened. Why is that?

112. Two boys, James and Harry, were riding their bikes up a hill. Suddenly, they spotted a quickly spreading fire. James said that they should go down the hill because they can escape the fire. Harry said that they should go up the hill because it will take more time for the fire to go uphill. Who is right and why?

Chapter 2 - Answers

The pocket has a hole in it.

Harry was bald.

D-A-Y

The three people are the grandfather, the father, and the son.

You draw a shorter line next to it.

A promise

Sarah had thrown the ball straight up.

When you add 2 to 11 o'clock, you get 1 o'clock.

Unsuccessfully

0. The question is: Are you asleep yet?

1. The barber

2. The word is starting.

    a. starting

    b. staring

    c. string

    d. sting

    e. sing

    f. sin

    g. in

    h. I

3. You find words that have a letter repeated twice.

4. Your name

5. The ostrich does not belong to the group because it cannot fly.

5. The day after tomorrow is the 26th.

7. The word is "Isle," You can add the letter "A" to it, and it becomes "Aisle." The word still pronounced the same way, but the meaning changes completely.

3. The word is DELETE.

9. Neutrons cannot have a positive charge. In fact, they don't have any charge at all.

0. You stop imagining.

1. The word is CARPET.

Chapter 2 - Answers

22. You have two because that is how many you took.

23. Because she took a picture of the sunset, she had to be facing west.

24. You need only one. You just need the last one to complete the building.

25. Because, I am a kiwi.

26. The word WALK is between the word PARK. Or, in other words, it is in the word PARK. Therefore, the phrase is "A walk in the park."

27. The man was a police officer.

28. Louie is drinking coffee. Anyone with two "E's" in their names is drinking tea while those with a single "E" are drinking coffee.

29. The letters represent the days of the week. The missing letter is "F."

30. All of them

31. Short

32. Yesterday, today, and tomorrow

33. The man saw the North Star. Using that fixed point, he was able to find where east, west, and south were.

34. The letter "w"

35. The person who had the biggest head

36. They have foals, which are baby horses.

37. The next letter is "D." Each of the letters is the first letter of 11 months.

38. It was still Mt. Everest. It just hadn't been discovered yet.

39. Their friend Wednesday did.

40. It wasn't raining.

41. Heroine

42. The word is NOON. It reads the same if you read it backwards and if you flip it over.

43. The man simply has to wait until night. Once the sun sets, he can leave the room through the first door.

44. Racecar is spelled the same backward or forward.

45. It is an envelope

46. You can only do it once. After that, you will be subtracting 5 from 95.

Chapter 2 - Answers

7. Tim was watching the tsunami on TV.

8. The entire paragraph is missing the letter "E," which is the most common letter in the English language.

9. The two people were facing each other.

0. The word is "keyboard." The first three letters refer to a key, which can open a lock. The last five letters spell board, the flat surface.

1. It is London!

    a. 1/4 of Leek is the letter "L."

    b. 2/5 of onion are the letters "ON."

    c. 1/9 of drumstick is the letter "D."

    d. 2/5 of onion is once again, the letters "ON."

2. The word is "snowball." The first word is snow, which is the white and soft object. The last word is ball, which is the round object that can roll on the ground.

3. Each word is missing the letter "I," which means that each of the words is MICE. The missing "I" is a reference to EYE. So, the sentence means "Three Blind Mice."

4. It will still take the cat 10 minutes.

5. You can fit just one. After that, the box is not empty anymore.

6. He has five. Each brother has the same sister.

7. The word "wrong"

8. She added holes to it.

9. The word is "Queue." If you remove the last four letters, you will still be able to pronounce it the same way – "Q."

0. The word is "weighty." If you remove the "Y" and the "W," then you have eight remaining.

1. The score for any football game always starts with zero! That's easy to predict.

2. The young girl ate corn. You remove the outer layer before cooking the inside.

3. The word is HURRY written in such a way that it starts at the bottom and goes up. In other words, the letters refer to the phrase "Hurry Up."

4. The letters all represent the word "eggs." But, they are scrambled. That means that the phrase you are looking for is "Scrambled Eggs."

Chapter 2 - Answers

65. A banana is 6 dollars. You are simply taking the number of letters in each fruit and then turning them into the price.

66. He used a pencil.

67. The outside

68. I finished in second place.

69. The boy was reading braille.

70. There are a total of four horses. They are standing in a square formation.

71. He did move 2 feet. He just moved his 2 feet!

72. Look backwards

73. He tore up one piece of paper and asked the king to tell what was under the remaining piece of paper. The king lifted it up and it showed "NO." The young man said, in front of the whole crowd, that obviously what he had torn had to have contained the "YES" word.

74. Follow the series below.

    a. DINER

    b. MINER

    c. MINES

    d. MINUS

    e. MENUS

75. You pour water into the hole. The ball will float to the top.

76. You simply pulled the plug in the bathtub.

77. Roosters do not lay eggs.

78. The plural form of deer is deer. Deers is incorrect.

79. The water was in a container.

80. Peter bought a candle and a box of matches. When he lit the candle, the entire room was filled with light.

81. It is possible if you could somehow fly at the speed of light.

82. There are exactly 12 seconds in a year - January 2nd, February 2nd, and so on until December 2nd.

83. You can use the toothpicks to spell the word "ten."

Chapter 2 - Answers

There are four "give." This means the four words say forgive!

It is because Ella dropped the ring on dried coffee grounds.

You choose the barber on the right. Since the barbers have to do each other's hair, barber on the left created bald patches while the barber on the right created shiny, ll-done hair.

Oil does not mix with water. He could not mix it well.

It was daytime.

The cars were moving toward each other but at different times. One car started at '0 a.m. while the other car started at 2:00 p.m.

Lunch and dinner

The doctor is the girl's father.

He was just running. He wasn't driving a vehicle.

Amber loves pumpkins. She only prefers to have food that grows on vines.

Pigs cannot look up at the sky. It is physically impossible for them to do so.

Salamanders do not belong in the group because they are classified as amphibians.

It is because dolphins don't sing. They click.

You take sand in order to make glass.

There is no air in space. Therefore, sound cannot travel in space.

John does not have any power. He was holding a battery and he charged it.

0.   The girl was returning a book she had borrowed. She was paying the overdue

1.   The three primary colors are red, yellow, and blue.
2.   The youngest son is not tall enough. He can press the ground floor button, but cannot press the 10th- floor button.
3.   He revealed a secret.
4.   The man saw the reflection of the moon in a lake or a small puddle of water.
5.   There was no unknown force. Adam had gone bungee jumping. There was an stic cord attached to him that pulled him to safety.
5.   They were born in two different locations and therefore, two different dates/ e zones.

Chapter 2 - Answers

107. The man was born in 1995 BC. When it was 1996, it was 1996 AD. Nearly 3,991 years had passed since the time he was born.

108. She has only three daughters – a brunette, a blonde, and a redhead.

109. If all the walls of the house are facing south, then the house is in the north pole. That means that the bear is white.

110. You will have written it 120 times. There are 10 fours in the one's place, 10 fours in the ten's place, and there are 100 fours in the hundred's place.

111. Die is the singular form of the word dice.

112. James is right. Fires usually travel in the direction of the ambient wind, which usually goes uphill.

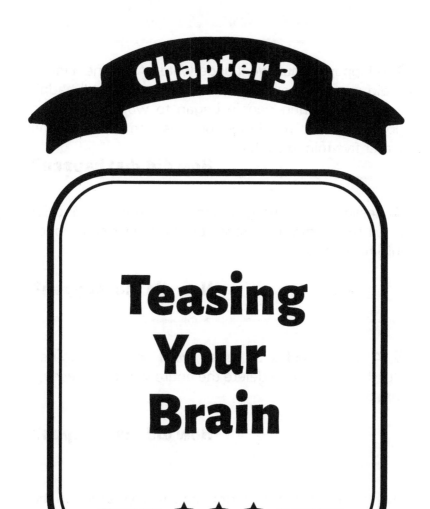

Chapter 3

Teasing Your Brain

★ ★ ★

"Who questions much, shall learn much, and retain much."

~ Francis Bacon

Chapter 3 - Questions

1. A hippopotamus went underwater. After one minute, it did not come out. After two minutes, it still hadn't come out. When people began to worry about the poor creature, the hippopotamus came out of the water five minutes later.

How did that happen?

2. Leslie took a string attached to an object and let it fall to the ground. However, the object came back into his hands.

How did that happen?

3. A man typed a 24-letter word on his computer. But, he was able to delete the entire word by pressing just two keys.

How did that happen?

4. In the middle of the night, Jim saw a creature on the ground. Suddenly, the creature became two. However, one of the two creatures was not moving while the other moved into the bushes.

How did that happen?

5. A young boy capitalized the first letter of a word and turned it from an object into a language.

How did that happen?

6. A boy saw a mushroom-like object floating on the water. When he touched it, he received quite a shock!

How did that happen?

7. A man created a line that was 2 feet long. He then easily removed 1 foot from the line and added a square.

How is that possible?

8. A boy was able to use the same three letters arranged in the same way to complete the following words: D E _ _ _ S T , S T _ _ _ , and P _ _ _ N T.

How did that happen?

9. In a clock, one single moving part, which is the second hand, is needed to complete a minute. However, John got a timepiece that required more than a hundred moving parts to complete a minute.

How did that happen?

10. There were two twins who were lying down beside a queen and a king. However, there was nobody in the room.

How did that happen?

11. A dog is tied to a leash that is 5 feet long. There is a bowl of delicious food 30 feet away. The dog still manages to reach the food.

How did that happen?

12. A man wanted to swim in the Dead Sea. But, when he jumped into it, he began to float.

How did that happen?

13. On Venus, the sun rises in the west and sets in the east.

How did that happen?

Long before toothpaste was
created, people used
to applycharcoal to their teeth
to brush them.

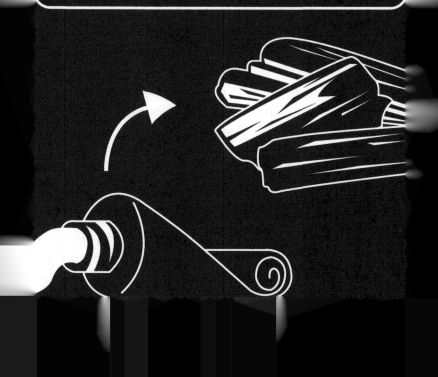

14. A man had a heart in his hands. Then, he suddenly had a diamond.

How did that happen?

15. A man goes to a pet store. He sees a parrot and the seller says that the parrot can repeat any word that the parrot hears. The man buys the parrot and takes it home. At home, the parrot does not repeat a single word that the man speaks.

How did that happen?

16. There was a bus driver who was going down a one-way road. He took a right turn when no right turn was allowed. He went through a building and came out on the other side.

How did that happen?

Chapter 3 - Questions

17. A driver had to navigate his car below a bridge. However, his car was one inch too tall. He still went under the bridge without getting a single scratch on the car.

How did that happen?

18. A cat decided to walk for five hours. At the end of those five hours, two of its legs had covered 5 kilometers while the other two had covered 5.5 kilometers.

How did that happen?

19. A man was sitting in a cabin in London. Three hours later, he stepped out of the cabin and he was in Paris!

How did that happen?

Chapter 3 - Questions

20. James was moving down a footpath, but for some reason, he was moving sideways. He then suddenly flipped around while continuing to move in the same direction. He kicked the ground, but he didn't lift off.

How did that happen?

21. There were two friends who wanted to find out which of their horses was slower. They were wondering how to solve this problem when they asked their third friend. The third friend said something and eventually, the two friends were able to find out which horse was slower.

How did that happen?

22. There was a piece of carrot, several pieces of coal, and a scarf lying near a tree. No one put them on the ground.

How did that happen?

23. A farmer had a bunch of nails and a hammerhead in his hands. He placed them in a large pond. After a few months, the hammerhead had grown.

How did that happen?

24. Tim entered the kitchen and saw a basket that had an orange, a pineapple, a lemon, a kiwi, and a strawberry. He then created invisible ink.

How did that happen?

FUN FACT

Did you know that the lips of a hippopotamus are quite big? How big? Well, they can be as wide as two feet!

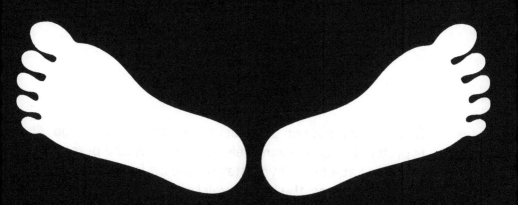

25. Why are 1995 pennies worth less than 2018 pennies?

26. A father and son come across a bridge. The bridge is pretty strong but extremely narrow. Only one person can cross at a time. If you stay on the bridge for longer than 20 seconds, the bridge will break. It takes exactly 20 seconds to reach the other side. The father and son together reached the other side at the same time.

How did that happen?

Chapter 3 - Questions

27. Two men approached a river but found only one single-person boat on the shore. However, they were both able to cross the river.

How did that happen?

---

28. There was once a farmer and his dog. One day, the farmer and the dog found themselves on the opposite sides of a large lake. The farmer called out to the dog and the dog calmly walked on the lake to reach the farmer!

How did that happen?

---

29. A young boy closed his eyes. When he opened them, he was in the middle of a forest and a bear was running toward him. He closed his eyes and opened them again. He was back in his room.

How did that happen?

---

30. A young boy was running away from a dragon. Suddenly, he was inside a car and racing against many other cars. Before he could win the race, he was in a football field trying to score a goal against the other team.

How did that happen?

Chapter 3 - Questions

31. There were two brothers who always hung out together. One day, they met their friend. Together, the two brothers and one friend became a unique group. They become something else entirely.

How did that happen?

32. There were three doctors. They all said that Mark is their brother. But Mark has no brothers.

How did that happen?

33. A man jumped out of a plane from nearly 30,000 feet. At first, he was falling down quite fast, but then he began to slow down a little. Finally, he landed on the ground without hurting himself.

How did that happen?

34. A person pushed a surface and it moved away from him. However, when he relaxed, the surface came back to him.

How is that possible?

35. A man saw a horse running across a field. He then saw a king run faster than the horse!

How did that happen?

FUN FACT

The first microwave oven
that was invented was as tall as
a refrigerator!

Chapter 3 - Questions

36. A man decided to run for 3 kilometers. However, even after finishing his run, he was still in the same spot.

How did that happen?

37. A young girl opened a glass door and stepped into a building. It was hot inside and there were many plants. But as soon as she stepped outside, there was nothing.

How did that happen?

FUN FACT

In Siberia, it can get so cold that
your breath can turn to ice
in front of your face.

38. Philip poured a liquid into a tumbler. He stirred the liquid using a spoon and then poured the liquid out. However, the liquid did not stick to the surface of the tumbler.

How did that happen?

39. A man was using a car when he stopped at a hotel. He then said that he had no more money left. After a few more stops, he shouted with joy, "I now have so much money with me!"

How did that happen?

40. A young man was walking down the road when he saw a pair of glowing eyes. Initially, he was frightened. Then he calmed down and approached the glowing eyes. He asked, "Would you like to be my friend?" The next day, he woke up in his room to find the eyes looking at him, but they were not glowing anymore.

How did that happen?

Chapter 3 - Answers

Hippopotamuses can hold their breath for up to five minutes!

Leslie was using a yo-yo.

The man used CTRL+backspace on the keyboard.

Jim saw a snake shedding its skin.

The word was "polish." If you capitalize the first letter, it becomes Polish, which is a language.

The boy touched a jellyfish.

The man was using a pencil and an eraser.

The boy used the letters A-R-E.

John got an hourglass. More than a hundred tiny grains of sand are required to complete a minute.

. They were the sizes of beds - two twin size, one queen size, and one king size.

. The leash itself was not tied to anything but the dog.

. If you jump into the Dead Sea, you won't sink to the bottom. You will be floating top.

. Venus spins in the opposite direction of Earth.

. The man was playing with a deck of cards.

. The parrot is deaf.

. The bus driver was not driving the bus; he was walking.

. The man removed some air from his tires.

. The cat was moving in circles. The inner legs cover less distance than the outer legs.

. The man was seated in an airplane cabin.

. James was riding a skateboard.

. The third friend told the other two to sit on each other's horses. Whoever wins so proves that their horse is slower.

. These were all objects from a melted snowman.

Chapter 3 - Answers

23. It was a hammerhead shark.

24. You can use lemon juice as invisible ink.

25. 1995 is not the year of the pennies but the number of pennies.

26. The father carried the son on his shoulders.

27. They approached the river from the opposite shores. They each found one boat on their shore.

28. The lake was frozen.

29. The young boy was dreaming. When he closed his eyes the first time, he had drifted off to sleep. When he closed his eyes a second time, it was in his dreams.

30. The young boy was playing a video game.

31. The two brothers were hydrogen. When they combined with oxygen, they were able to turn into H20 (water).

32. The three doctors were Mark's sisters.

33. The man used a parachute.

34. The person was doing push-ups.

35. The man was watching a game of chess.

36. The man was running on a treadmill. Acceptable answer: The man was running in place.

37. The young girl had stepped into a greenhouse.

38. Philip poured mercury into the tumbler. Mercury does not stick to surfaces easily.

39. The man was playing Monopoly.

40. The young man had come across a cat. Cats' eyes can "glow" in the dark, which can make them scary. The young man then took the cat home. The next day, the cat looked at him without "glowing" eyes.

Chapter 4

Jumbling It Up!

★ ★ ★ ★

"Any book that helps a child to form a habit of reading, to make reading one of his deep and continuing needs, is good for him."

~ Maya Angelou

These words are jumbled up. All you need to do is follow the clues provided under each question to help you reach the correct answer. For this section, you can use a pen and paper if you feel you would like to try rearranging the words. However, the best challenge is to try and guess the word without using pen and paper. In fact, if you follow the clues, you may not need any additional tools.

1. NANSVAA

Clues: This is not a living thing. In fact, it is a type of environment where living things grow. There are a lot of trees in this environment and it has another nickname - "tropical grasslands." You usually find large groups of animals here. In fact, you can easily spot lions and elephants in this environment.

2. OHGDYNER

Clues: It is something that is very light! It is present in the sun. It is the first of its kind. You can easily find it on a table.

FUN FACT

There are more muscles in
a caterpillar than there are
in a human being.

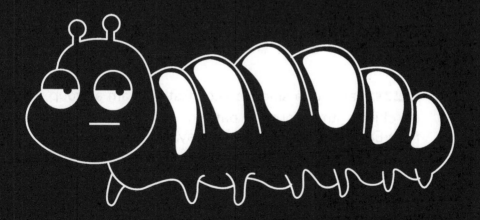

3.   E B O O S S I R M

Clues: They are factories, but they are not buildings that you find outside! They are usually producing stuff to help tiny little things inside you. They contain subunits and each subunit has something called RNA.

4.   I C T R F I N O

Clues: Because of this, you can rub your hands together to produce some heat. If anything tries to enter Earth from space, then you know they have to face this. If two objects slide against each other, they slow down because of this.

5.   E L N S A T L O S C N T O I

Clues: I am not a single object. Rather, I am a group of objects that form a pattern. You can see me from Earth, but I am quite far away. You won't be able to see me during the day. I have many friends and some of them are quite far away. If you need to see my friends, then you might have to use an object that can help you see far.

6. UFMER

Clues: It is something that is in your body. It is the largest of its kind. You need it to move forward, backward, and sideways. It is quite strong.

7. DESOAITRS

Clues: These objects are rocks, but you don't find them anywhere on Earth. Some of them are quite small, but others can be bigger than a city. You wouldn't want them on Earth. If you do, then you should make sure that they land softly even though that is not possible.

8. LCOHRYLPOLH

Clues: You cannot find this in human beings. In fact, you cannot find this in any animal, fish, or bird. Yet, it is present in living things. It is related to sunlight.

9. NIRLCAOTAEEC

Clues: When you think of things that are moving, then you think of this word. It really is not an object, neither is it something you can hold. However, it describes the nature of objects, especially objects in motion. When changes occur in objects, then this word is the result.

FUN FACT

The human eye is capable of
processing more than 120
million bits of information
every second.

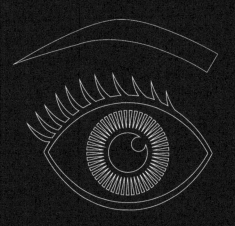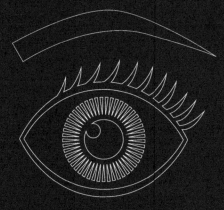

10. S O P O S N I R C

Clues: You might think that these are insects, but they really are not. However, they are capable of leaving behind quite a sting. The smaller they are, the more dangerous they are.

11. E N C O S O A L V

Clues: They are a large opening, but not one you would like to enter. Their contents are quite hot. In fact, you will feel the heat the closer you get to them. They are like gateways into the Earth, but people don't usually get into them. They spew out something that can cause a lot of destruction.

12. T N E N E R T I

Clues: This word does not represent a living thing, nor is it a physical object. You and many other people in the world use it. It is a source of fun and information. You can even say hello to your family by using it.

13. E O O N Z

Clues: There is much oxygen in this region. It is almost like a protective layer, although it cannot be formed without the help of the sun. Surprisingly, even though it needs the sun to create it, it also protects from the sun as well!

14. E E M R P A

Clues: This word is a form of measurement. You cannot find it on any ruler, but it does indicate something. To be more specific, it indicates something that is in a current form.

15. U E L C S E O M L

Clues: They cannot be easily seen using the naked eye. However, they are present in every single object in the word. They come in different forms. Each form creates something unique. One of their forms is actually important for our lives.

16. A U T R L A T N A

Clues: I walk on eight legs, and I easily frighten many people. I am part of a whole family of living things. Some of my family members might be living in your home! I am quite hairy, which is also one of the frightening things about me. I can be anywhere from 3 inches to 10 inches big. I think the bigger I am the more people avoid me.

17. C T M R C N M I A O H O O

Clues: This word refers to colors. But it does not refer to just any set of colors. The word indicates all the colors of a particular hue. For example, it could refer to light red, dark red, or even deep red, but it indicates a specific type of color.

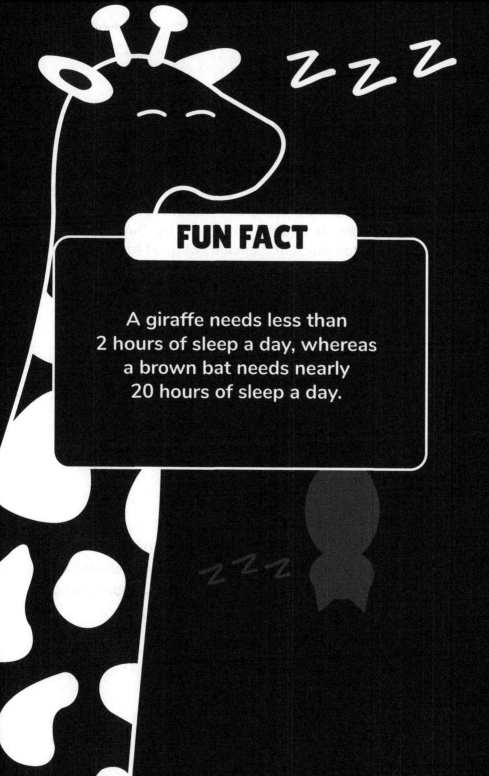

FUN FACT

A giraffe needs less than
2 hours of sleep a day, whereas
a brown bat needs nearly
20 hours of sleep a day.

18. STRYORCEADHBA

Clues: When you think of these things, you are not exactly thinking of an object. They can be quite starchy, and they are found within your body. You can actually feel quite energetic by having them, although too much of them are not good for you. They are also known to provide structure to many animals and plants.

19. CTATINL ANEOAC

Clues: These two words refer to something that is present in large quantities. In its group, it is the saltiest. It can carry many big and small objects. It can also allow many big and small objects to pass through it.

20. CHRMTMIPOAE

Clues: This word is the name of a type of object that is found everywhere on Earth. Some of these objects are above ground, while many are buried underground. They are formed by extreme heat and pressure.

21. AOUPRE

Clues: This word refers to an object that goes around an even bigger object. The bigger object is called a planet. Among the planets in our solar system, one planet is the biggest of them all and it has this object going around it.

22. MIEGMSTNA

Clues: It is a kind of force that exists in nature. In fact, one can say that it is a very important force. attracted to each other. It is also the reason why a compass needle points in the right direction.

23. YKTURE

Clues: This word refers to a country that is also an animal. Regarding the country, it forms a connection between Europe and the Middle East. Regarding the animal, it is quite famous in certain countries as it is used during the holidays.

24. Y R B A T R E W R S

Clues: This word refers to something that has always been thought of as a berry, but it actually isn't. You can find these objects in your local store. They can sometimes be sweet as well.

25. C T I I I O B N T A S

Clues: They can be solid, or they can be in liquid form. You don't find them all around you. You can only get them in special places. They are mainly given to protect your health. In many cases, you might have to visit the doctor first.

26. M N T L U I A P

Clues: This word refers to a kind of metal. It is the third in the tenth column. What kind of column? Oh, that would be giving away too much! Normally, it can be quite silvery and shiny.

27. G I E R G N N D A

Clues: This word refers to a type of activity that human beings do. When humans require food, they do this. It can produce different kinds of foods. Some of them are sweet while others are not.

FUN FACT

There is a waterfall in Hawaii that can sometimes go up instead of down.

28. A R E B C T I A

Clues: You find many of these almost everywhere on the planet. Some of them are also found on you and inside you! Some of them can be quite deadly, while others are really helpful.

29. T L I A T U E O V R L

Clues: This word is a type of color but is one that you cannot see. The only way you can see it is if you were using special instruments. If you had to compare it to one of the primary colors, you would think of the color blue.

30. H G E E A T N L V W

Clues: This word refers to a type of measurement. It's a measurement of an unseen force and it usually requires two points. The unit it measures has an up and down movement almost like a wave.

FUN FACT

In an ancient ruin in China, noodles that were nearly four thousand years old were discovered.

Chapter 4 - Answers

1. Savanna

2. Hydrogen

3. Ribosomes

4. Friction

5. Constellations

6. Femur

7. Asteroids

8. Chlorophyll

9. Acceleration

10. Scorpions

---

11. Volcanoes

12. Internet

13. Ozone

14. Ampere

15. Molecules

16. Tarantula

17. Monochromatic

18. Carbohydrates

19. Atlantic Ocean

20. Metamorphic

---

21. Europa

22. Magnetism

23. Turkey

24. Strawberry

25. Antibiotics

26. Platinum

27. Gardening

28. Bacteria

29. Ultraviolet

30. Wavelength

Did you enjoy the book?

If you did, we are ecstatic. If not, please write your complaint to us and we will ensure we fix it.

If you're feeling generous, there is something important that you can help me with – tell other people that you enjoyed the book.

Ask a grown-up to write about it on Amazon. When they do, more people will find out about the book. It also lets Amazon know that we are making kids around the world enjoy reading and working out riddles. Even a few words and ratings would go a long way.

If you have any ideas or riddles that you think are interesting, please let us know. We would love to hear from you. Our email address is -

riddleland@riddlelandforkids.com

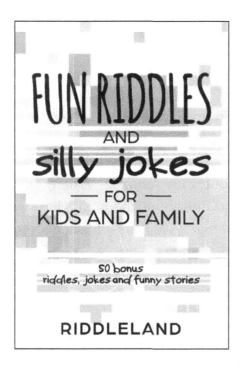

SCAN ME

https://pixelfy.me/riddlelandbonus

Thank you for buying this book. As a token of our appreciation, we would like to offer a special bonus - a collection of 50 original jokes, riddles and funny stories.

CONTEST

Would you like your jokes and riddles to be featured in our next book?

We are having a contest to see who are the smartest or funniest boys and girls in the world!

1) Creative and Challenging Riddles
2)Tickle Your Funny Bone Contest

Parents, please email us your child's "original" riddle or joke, **and he or she could win a $25 Amazon gift card and be featured in our next book.**

Here are the rules:

1) We are looking for super challenging riddles and extra funny jokes

2) Jokes and riddles Must be 100% original - Not something discovered on the internet.

3) You can submit both a joke and a riddle as they are two separate contests.

4) Don't get help from your parents unless they are as funny as you are.

5) Winners will be announced via email or our Facebook group – Riddleland for kids

6) P

7) Email us at <u>Riddleland@riddlelandforkids.com</u>

Other Fun Books By Riddleland
Riddles Series

Try Not to Laugh Challenge
Joke Series

Would You Rather Series

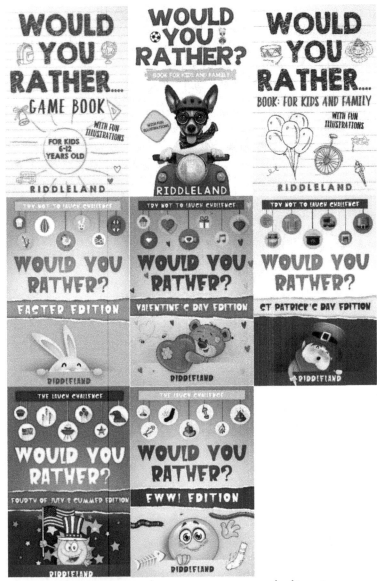

Get them on Amazon or our website at
www.riddlelandforkids.com

About Riddleland

Riddleland is a mum + dad run publishing company. We are passionate about creating fun and innovative books to help children develop their reading skills and fall in love with reading. If you have suggestions for us or want to work with us, shoot us an email at

riddleland@riddlelandforkids.com

Our family's favorite quote

"Creativity is an area in which younger people have a tremendous advantage since they have an endearing habit of always questioning past wisdom and authority."

– Bill Hewlett.